TEACHINGS OF JESUS CHRIST

OTHER TITLES IN THIS SERIES

TEACHINGS OF JESUS CHRIST

AJANTA CHAKRAVARTY

RIDER

LONDON · SYDNEY · AUCKLAND · JOHANNESBURG

1 3 5 7 9 10 8 6 4 2

First published in 1997 by Shishti Publishers, India.
This edition published in 1998 by Rider, an imprint of
Ebury Press
Random House UK Ltd
Random House
20 Vauxhall Bridge Road
London SW1V 2SA

Random House Australia (Pty) Ltd
20 Alfred Street
Milsons Point, Sydney
New South Wales, 2016 Australia

Random House New Zealand Limited
18 Poland Road, Glenfield
Auckland 10, New Zealand

Random House South Africa (Pty) Limited
Endulini, 5A Jubilee Road
Parktown 2193, South Africa

Random House UK Limited Reg. No. 954009

Papers used by Rider Books are natural, recyclable products made from wood grown in sustainable forests.

Printed and bound in Great Britain by CPD, Wales

A CIP catalogue record for this book is available from the British Library

ISBN 0-7126-7192-7

space. Those which survived went through many trials and tribulations, each tempering its core values for greater robustness. Their Masters, often coming at the darkest hour, brought messages of hope. Of good sense. Of homespun, sensible practices which could be adopted by all, irrespective of birth and position. Unfortunately, the passage of time invariably obscured these precepts. The primary cause for this was that the language forms underwent spatial and temporal changes, restructuring and reinterpreting. These variations proceeded to filter into common usage according to their ability of easing Man's understanding. Over time, the regular languages changed their forms so radically that the scriptural languages were rendered impotent. Thus the wisdom inherent in them was lost to new generations.

This series of books attempts to rediscover and reinterpret some of the teachings from the scriptures of a few mainstream religions, in a form suitable for absorption by the twentieth century person poised on the threshold of the twenty-first. The kind of world we will make then will depend to a great extent on the wisdom that precedes every small or big decision. Perhaps the information in this book will help in reinforcing the learning for making a better and more beautiful life space for humanity at large.

TEACHINGS OF JESUS CHRIST

Jesus Christ was born to Joseph, a humble carpenter, and his wife Mary. He was born in a lowly manger on a cold winter night in the town of Bethlehem. His parents were too poor to secure lodgings for the night. That night a bright star shone in the sky and guided three wise men from the East who came to pay homage to one who would set an eternal example for the world through his supreme sacrifice.

When Jesus grew up, he was acknowledged as the Messiah by John the Baptist, a reformer known for his fiery zeal. Jesus led a life of exemplary humility but his teachings were divine, touching a primordial chord deep within ordinary men and women, bowed down by the laws of the land. He espoused a simple religion, bereft of rituals and expensive trappings. His way was that of love, truth and compassion for all, irrespective of position or status. Many miracles were ascribed to him. His followers called him the Son of God. This, together with his determined resistance to temples and moneylenders brought the wrath of the establishment on his head.

Many descriptions exist of his trial and crucifixion. But mere words fail to describe the anguish and poignancy of his last journey, stumbling and falling under the weight of the cross, a crown of thorns drawing blood from his temples while his terror-stricken disciples lurked behind the jeering crowd to avoid meeting his gaze. Who can picture the agony of nails piercing through flesh and blood, of being suspended from the shrieking red-hot torment of crucified hands. Yet the only words that passed his lips were, "Forgive them Father, for they know not what they do."

Christ's teachings endured among his disciples who went through much tribulation to establish Christianity. But the Holy Bible dates from long before Christ. The present-day versions offer both the old testament and the new. Much has been culled from the Hebrew, Greek and Aramaic versions. Under the flowing, graceful words of the Bible lie homespun, down-to-earth truths. An effort has been made here to present some of these homilies for the easy comprehension of the pressed for time, modern-day reader.

To shun evil is to understand the wisdom of the Lord.

Put on the robe of righteousness and justice in all your affairs.

Be the eyes to the blind and feet to the lame.

Do you shun a man once he loses the vigour of his limbs?

Does He not see my deeds and count my footsteps?

The same One gave form to my servant and to me within our mothers' wombs, and in the same way.

Should a young man fear the old, not daring to speak of what he knows?

God speaks – now in one way, now another, though men may not perceive it.

While men slumber, He speaks in their dreams. The righteous remember on waking while others forget.

Can he, who hates justice, govern?

No shadow is deep enough to hide the evil-doer from His eyes.

Your wickedness does not affect God but only men like yourself.

Your righteousness affects not God but only the sons of men.

Time is wasted when words are multiplied without knowledge.

Blessed is the man who does not sit in the gallery of mockers or walk in the counsel of the wicked.

Man's throat is an open grave when with his tongue he speaks deceit.

Day after day, the skies pour forth speech and night after night, they display their knowledge. We miss it because we do not look up.

Do not be envious of those who do wrong,
for like grass, they will soon wither.

Do not fret when others carry out wicked schemes successfully. Like green plants, they will soon wither away.

Man piles up wealth not knowing who will finally benefit.

Does God need your offerings to be able to eat and dress? Give instead to the poor.

Set a guard over your mouth and keep a watch over the doorway of your lips lest you speak words of dishonesty.

God is in heaven but his idols are made by men with petty ambitions.

Let the wise also listen and add to their learning.

Try not to be wise in your own eyes.

Do not say `Come back tomorrow' to another if you can help him today.

See the wisdom of the ant! It has neither rules nor overseers, yet it stores its provisions diligently while others play.

Rebuke a mocker and he will hate you. But rebuke a wise man and see him love you.

He who ignores corrections leads others astray.

A kind man benefits himself while a cruel man brings harm unto himself.

A beautiful woman who shows no discretion is like a gold ring in a pig's snout.

A fool shows his annoyance at once but a prudent man overlooks an insult.

A man's riches may ransom his life but a poor man hears no threats.

A gentle answer turns away wrath but a harsh word may stir up anger.

He who loves to quarrel builds a highway to destruction.

Speak judiciously. Even a fool may be considered discerning if he holds his tongue.

A rebuke impresses a man of discernment more than does a hundred lashes a fool.

It is not good to be hasty and miss the way.

A quarrelsome wife is like a constant drip.

The glory of the young is their strength and grey hair the splendour of the old.

If a man shuts his ears to the cry of the poor,
he too will cry out and not be heeded.

Do not eat the food of a man who is always counting its cost.

By wisdom is a house built and through understanding is it established.

As dead flies can give even perfume a bad smell, so a little folly outweighs wisdom and honour.

Whoever digs a pit may fall into it himself.

A scoundrel is he who stirs up dissension among brothers.

Can a man scoop fire into his lap without burning his clothes?

Better to be nobody and have a servant than pretend to be somebody and have no food.

Better a dry crust with peace than a house full of feasting with strife.

Dishonest money dwindles away. He who gathers money little by little makes it grow.

You will be judged by the same measure as you judge others.

Why do you look at the speck of sawdust in your brother's eye and pay no attention to the plank in your own eye?

Seek. Then only will you find.

If you know how to give presents to your children, how much more will our father in heaven give to those who ask him.

Do unto others what you would have them do to you.

Watch out for false prophets who come in sheep's clothing but inwardly are like fierce wolves.

Does a thorn bush grow grapes that you expect a false prophet to lead you to heaven.

A wise man builds his house on rock while a fool builds on sand.

It is not the healthy who need a doctor but the sick. So does a prophet call not to the righteous alone, but also to the sinners.

The man with two Genics should share with him who has none.

An honest answer is like a kiss on the lips.

Do not exalt yourself in a King's presence. It is better for him to say "Come up here."

Do not betray another man's confidence.

The man who boasts of gifts he does not give is like a cloud without rain.

Even gentle tongue can break bones.

If you find honey, do not eat too much of it or you will vomit.

Like one who takes away a garment an a cold day is one who sings songs to a heavy heart.

Better to live in a corner of the roof than share a house with a quarrelsome person.

Like a city whose walls are broken down is a man who lacks self-control.

As a dog returns to its vomit, so a fool repeats his folly.

A passerby who meddles in a quarrel not his own is like one who seizes a dog by the ear.

Without gossip, a quarrel dies dawn.

Like a coat of glaze over earthenware are fervent lips with an evil heart.

Do not boast about tomorrow for you do not know what the day may bring forth.

Everyone is the friend of a man who gives presents.

Zeal without knowledge is not much good.

The first to present his case seems right till another comes forward and questions him.

A fool's mouth is his undoing.

possible. Language gave him the means to communicate his thoughts, his feelings, his enquiries with others. His superior brain enabled the processing of loose, unstructured information into systematic forms. This was knowledge, the most powerful tool at his command. He could use it for harmony, growth and peace or for wanton annihilation. What he needed were guidelines for implementing his knowledge. He sought the power of wisdom. And once again, he turned, both to the forces outside to understand the mysteries of nature and within, to know the truth of his very being. He wanted to learn from the Masters who had drunk deep of the springs of wisdom and on whose teachings were founded the great religions, the pathways of discernment.

It must be noted that many religions have come into being and almost as many have disappeared without trace. They could not measure up to the changing demands of life the 'vital elan', and his quest was both in the physical world outside and the spiritual world within himself. The last gave rise to religion.

It is often thought that primordial man was a not-so-clever animal, who blindly worshipped the forces of nature – the rocks, trees, streams, clouds and the stars. Many have expressed doubts about organized religion on account of its being an atavistic throwback to the dark ages of the past. In today's world of fast-paced determinism, religion is often publicly scorned but privately engaged in to propitiate the very same forces that may in some way make life space more acceptable to us. And in this cauldron of conflicting desires and ambitions, the true significance of religion and the religious teachings and precepts get lost.

Man's search for tools with which to master his environment led to science. But prior to that, he had evolved language, without which no development would have been

He who is full loathes honey, but to the hungry even bitter tastes sweet.

Better a neighbour nearby than a brother far away.

The wicked man flees though no one pursues.

There is a time to embrace and a time to refrain.

A good name is better than a fine perfume.

Wisdom makes one wise man more powerful than ten rulers in a city.

No man knows when his hour will come.

Wisdom is better than the weapons of war.

Preface

The origin of life on earth is a contentious issue between scientists and believers. Scientists search for the truth, trying to prove its existence through rigorous experimentation, leaving no room for ambiguities. Believers, on the other hand take the existence of the Supreme Truth as granted; the rest follows thereafter with irrefutable logic.

What is generally overlooked is that between these conflicting views, there is a definite common factor about the beginning of life, the coming into existence of living matter. This is the manifestation of the 'life-force' or what has been described by many as the 'vital elan'. This force must have a 'life space' around it to provide for its sustenance and reproduction. The two must fit precisely and harmoniously for life to grow, flourish and evolve into its many different forms.

There were calamities too. The iceage, the submergences, earthquakes, tornadoes, avalanches, and the volcanic eruptions changed life space so dramatically that entire species were wiped out. There were other disasters, less dramatic but of no less magnitude. Exhaustion of natural food resources, spoiling of natural habitat, and overcrowding of life space led to large-scale disasters. The changes in environment meant that the vital elan had two options, either to adapt to the changes or be annihilated. Very often it was the latter because the species lacked the ability to adjust to the oncoming changes and reorient themselves until it was too late.

When man finally appeared on earth, he was as exposed to all the vagaries of life space as other species. But he was intelligent. He could observe, deduce and apply his mind to the core of his thinking to harness the life space rather than be driven by it. He searched actively for means of enhancing

Dishonest money dwindles away.

Fools mock at making amends for sins.

Whoever heeds correction shows prudence.

He who walks with the wise grows wise.

A companion of fools suffers harm.

Righteousness exalts a nation.

With humility comes wisdom.

He who scorns instruction, pays for it.

The way of the unfaithful is hard.

A heart at peace gives life to the body but envy rots the bones.

The wicked street about freely when what is vile is honoured among men.

For lack of guidance a nation may fall.

Lazy hands make a man poor.

Do not envy wicked men and desire their company.

A poor man is shunned by all his relatives and friends.